Halloween

BY
Cass R. Sandak

CRESTWOOD HOUSE
New York

Library of Congress Cataloging-in-Publication Data
Sandak, Cass R.
  Halloween

  p. cm. — (Holidays)
  Includes bibliographical references.
  SUMMARY: Presents the history and customs of Halloween.
  1. Halloween — Juvenile literature. [1. Halloween] I. Title. II. Series: Holidays
  GT4965.S23   1990   394.2'683—dc20   89-25396   CIP
  ISBN 0-89686-500-2   AC

Photo Credits
Cover: Photo Researchers: (John Dommers)
Journalism Services: (Chris Marona) 4; (J.J. Clark) 31; 14, 44
DRK Photo: (N.H. Cheatham) 7, 40; (D. Cavagnaro) 11, 23, 32, 34; (Stanley Breeden) 20; (Daniel R.
    Krasemann) 27; (J. Wengle) 37
Culver Pictures, Inc.: 8, 12, 15, 16, 17, 38, 43
Berg & Associates: (R.L. Goddard) 19; (Margaret C. Berg) 28

Macmillan Publishing Company
866 Third Avenue
New York, NY 10022
Collier Macmillan Canada, Inc.

CRESTWOOD HOUSE

Printed in the United States

First Edition

10 9 8 7 6 5 4 3 2 1

Contents

With its witches, spiders, and spells, Halloween is a time when people enjoy being scared.

A Fun and Fearsome Holiday

Halloween is probably the most fun holiday of the year. Some people dress up in costumes and carve jack-o'-lanterns. Others go to Halloween parties. They may play traditional Halloween games that date back hundreds of years. Many children go from house to house trick-or-treating.

Halloween has both a playful and a fearsome side. Many of the scary aspects of Halloween come from earlier times. Halloween is one of our oldest holidays. Centuries ago, people celebrated the holiday as a festival dedicated to the Lord of Darkness and Death. Witches, ghosts, and goblins come from this time. Halloween traditions go far back in time, long before the time of Christ. Our modern Halloween customs combine ancient Celtic and Roman traditions with more recent Christian beliefs.

The Celtic Samhain

Halloween comes from a time when people lived close to nature. In late October in the Northern Hemisphere, the sun sets earlier each day. Days become short and nights grow long. Autumn winds begin to howl. Leaves change colors and drop off trees. These are signs of the coming winter.

Long ago, people hated winter. The sun did not shine much. Plants withered. Because there was little food, it was a hard time. People who were old or sick might die. Darkness and death were on everyone's minds as they looked to winter with dread.

About 3,000 years ago, people called Celts lived in the British Isles, France, and in other parts of Europe. This was long before Christianity, so the Celts were pagans. This means that they worshiped the sun, the moon, and the forces of nature. Their priests were called Druids.

Each year on the night of October 31, the Celts had a festival called Samhain. The name *Samhain* probably means summer's end. The holiday was a time to remember the Celtic god of darkness and death. Samhain lasted until sunset on November 2. The Samhain festival was a time of bonfires, special foods, and games.

The Samhain celebration took place at almost the same time that farmers had their harvest festival. The night of October 31 was the end of summer and the start of winter. It also marked the beginning of the Celtic New Year on November 1.

Late autumn is the season of gathering darkness. As winter approaches, the sun seems to get weaker. The Celts believed supernatural forces were most powerful during this time. These unseen forces were thought to cause the changes in the seasons.

During the Celtic Samhain festival, it was believed that the Lord

The ancient Celts celebrated a good fall harvest with a festival called Samhain. Today, people hold special events like this Halloween Festival, where a pumpkin patch is on display.

of Death opened up the gates of the underworld. The spirits of dead people left their graves. At that time, they could return to roam the earth or visit their homes and families.

Other kinds of goblins and demons also wandered. People looked for the ghosts of loved ones on the night of Samhain. They also left food for them because they did not want the spirits to be angry and do them harm. Many people wore costumes to avoid being recognized by unfriendly ghosts. To keep spirits away, people lit fires and lanterns.

Roman soldiers arrive at Stonehenge just in time to stop Druid priests from sacrificing a woman to the gods.

The Celts did not like the dark winter. In order to please the gods of sunlight and darkness, the Druids made sacrifices. They burned animals and crops on large bonfires. The warm light of these fires was supposed to attract good spirits. The Celts also wanted the evil powers to let the sun's strength return. People, too, sometimes were burned in the great fires. Often criminals or prisoners of war were burned. At other times, the Druids drew lots to find victims for the human sacrifices.

The Celtic midwinter festival of Yul marked the sun's acceptance of the priests' sacrifices at Samhain. Yul came about the time of our Christmas celebration. The sun would return and the people would survive. After December 21, the days gradually start to lengthen again and the earth starts eventually to grow warmer. This was a time of rejoicing. Spring would be on its way at the end of the long winter.

A Roman Celebration

The Romans first came to Britain around 50 B.C. In the first century A.D., they made the island part of their empire. The Romans who came to Britain brought many of their customs with them. They also changed some of the customs they found there.

In the centuries before Christ, the Romans, like the Celts, had an autumn festival. It came at the same time of year as the Celtic Samhain. The Romans called this festival Pomona. It honored their harvest goddess of the same name. Fruits, especially apples, were sacred to Pomona. Many Halloween customs and games that feature apples, apple peelings, or nuts probably date from this time. Pomona was a much gentler holiday than Samhain. There was nothing terrifying about Pomona.

At the end of October, the Romans celebrated another festival, called Feralia. It was a day devoted to prayers for the dead. Originally, Feralia had been intended to honor the memory of those who had died while serving the Roman Empire. But eventually the holiday became a day to remember all dead people. In time, the festivals and customs of Feralia, Pomona, and the Celtic Samhain all became linked.

All Hallows' Even

The traditions we associate with Halloween began hundreds of years before Christianity. But the name *Halloween* itself comes from the Christian feast of All Saints' Day. Halloween is a shortened form of All Hallows' Even. Halloween is the night before All Saints' Day, a holy day celebrated by the Christian Church on November 1. *Hallow* is an Old English word that means a saint or something holy.

A saint is a holy person who has died and whose soul has gone to heaven. Some saints have their own special days set by the Church. But many saints do not, and All Saints' Day, on November 1, is the day to remember all these saints—both those whose names are known and those whose names are not.

People of most religions remember their dead in one way or another. For many hundreds of years, Celtic and Roman people all over Europe had held their festivals for the dead on the night of October 31.

When Christianity spread throughout Europe, the Church gave the old Samhain and Feralia observances a new meaning. This night became the eve of All Saints' Day. All Saints' Day first became a churchwide holiday in A.D. 837.

People also wanted to remember the dead who were not saints. And so November 2 became All Souls' Day. On All Souls' Day, many people still pray for the souls of dead loved ones. Often they go to special church services. Sometimes they visit the graves of relatives and friends. They may decorate these graves with flowers or wreaths.

On All Souls' Day, people pray for the souls of their dead friends and relatives.

11

A Night for Witches and Witchcraft

By the time Samhain had become Halloween, the old Celtic religion had been largely replaced by Christianity. In 1484, Pope Innocent VIII finally outlawed the old religion. He believed it was connected with witchcraft. The word *witch* comes from the Old English *wicce*. It means wise woman. Witchcraft stands for both the power of witches and the practice of magic.

Witches were respected women at one time. They were consulted about many important matters. They healed the sick because they knew about uses for herbs and other plants. They also knew about the moon and the stars. They knew the secrets of nature.

The Christian religion did not allow witchcraft. The Church associated witches with the forces of evil and Satan. But witches continued to meet secretly in forests and fields. On moonlit nights they wore black clothes so they could not be seen. That is why pictures of witches always show them dressed in black. The cone-shaped hats that witches in pictures often wear were once a popular style worn by many women.

Long ago, people believed witches could ride on broomsticks. When witches gathered at their meetings, they often leapt over fires on their broomsticks. People who saw this dance thought they saw the witches flying. And the witches themselves believed they were flying because their minds were confused by the potions they brewed and drank.

In those times, anyone who was the least bit odd might be thought to be a witch. A lonely old woman who mumbled or cackled to herself could easily be muttering magic spells. *Spell* is an Old

Three witches in William Shakespeare's *Macbeth* chant over a deadly brew.

English word that means something said or chanted. In time it came to mean a curse or enchantment. People thought witches could cause fires, storms, and sickness by saying certain words.

Witches collected all sorts of odd ingredients for casting their spells—strange herbs, bat wings, animal insides, and parts of corpses. All of these things might come in handy for working a particular bit of magic.

In order to injure other people, a witch might make a wax doll. This doll stood for her victim. The witch might use a lock of hair, a nail clipping, or a piece of clothing from the victim. This would give the wax doll the personality of the person the witch wished to harm. Then the witch stuck the doll with pins or harmed it in some way. Supposedly this also harmed the person that the doll represented.

Witches, voodoo dolls, gremlins, and a devil dance in a old woodcut.

Witches swirl away into the night with their furry familiars in this drawing by Arthur Rackham.

Early settlers brought the belief in witchcraft to America. In 1692, in Salem, Massachusetts, ten young girls claimed a black servant named Tituba was a witch. They said she had possessed them with evil spirits, making them ill. The serving woman had been born in the West Indies and knew about the African voodoo rituals and black magic practiced there. She had often entertained the girls with her stories of island magic.

People in and around Salem listened to the girls. They thought there might be other witches in the colony. They forced the girls to accuse other people in Salem of witchcraft. The girls gave the names of hundreds of people. Those accused were thrown into jail. Many of them were put on trial and unjustly convicted of the crime of witchcraft. Most people believed what the girls said, including the judges. About 20 women, thought to be witches, were hanged.

One of history's most fascinating characters, Joan of Arc, was put to death as a witch. This happened more than 250 years before the

Women accused of practicing witchcraft were once burned alive at the stake.

Joan of Arc, the young shepherdess who led the French army to many victories, was accused of being a witch and burned at the stake.

Salem witch trials. A poor farm girl, Joan claimed angelic voices regularly spoke to her. The voices told her she would lead the French army. The army would win over the English, who then controlled most of France.

As long as the armies she led won battles, the French didn't care what Joan believed. But when the French lost, they became angry and turned against her. They sold her to the English as a captive. After an unfair trial, Joan of Arc was declared a witch. In 1429 she was burned at the stake in the town square of Rouen. Five centuries later, after years of investigation, the Roman Catholic Church declared Joan of Arc a saint. The Church realized Joan had been treated unfairly. They declared that the voices she heard had actually come from God.

A witch was believed to have sold herself to the Devil by making a special pact with him. As a sign that she was the Devil's own, the Devil bit her on some part of the body. This bite was called the witch's mark. Any woman might be proved a witch if her accusers found a wart, a mole, or any sort of blemish on her skin. At a time when hygiene left much to be desired, few people could be entirely free of insect bites or small skin infections.

According to popular belief, witches held one of their two main meetings, or sabbats, on Halloween night. At their great sabbats of Halloween and May Eve, witches were said to dance on hilltops with goblins and imps. Satan himself was believed to be present, sometimes playing the bagpipes or castanets made from dead men's bones.

As a safeguard against witches, people hung special charms outside their houses and barns, especially on Halloween. These charms might be the crossed branches of juniper and ash. An iron horseshoe or a string of garlic bulbs was also said to guard against witches' powers.

Black Cats, Bats, and Other Halloween Animals

The animals associated with Halloween are the animals connected to witchcraft. Witches almost always had familiars. These were pet animals that were believed to be demons. People thought a witch could take the shape of her familiar whenever she wanted.

Most often the animal was a cat. The cat might be white or brown

Is this black cat a friendly feline or a witch's familiar? A lost soul or a harmless pet?

or any other color. But at night, when witches usually went out to work their evil spells, any dark-colored cat looks black. And so the black Halloween cat came to be. Cats are quiet and mysterious. They seem perfect for Halloween. Long ago, the black cat was associated with Hecate, the goddess of witchcraft in ancient Greek mythology. The Celts believed the souls of wicked people were often reincarnated as black cats.

Sometimes the witch's familiar was an imp. An imp was a type of demon who helped a witch perform her magic. The imp could take

This blossom bat may look innocent, but its ancestors had reputations as bloodsucking vampires and were thought to be ingredients in witches' brews.

the shape of a dog, a hen, a cat, or any other animal. It could even be a small insect. Witches thought that imps' movements gave important clues about how to cast spells.

The owl is another Halloween animal. In ancient Rome, owls were believed to be evil, although in Greece they were considered holy. With its piercing shriek, the screech owl was particularly dreaded in medieval Europe. People thought witches often took the form of owls. To hear an owl's call was a sign that someone was about to die.

Because they are so unappealing and also because they fly, bats, too, became symbols of Halloween. Witches often used bats' blood in making ointments and potions. They frequently put bat wings and insides into their brews. And old pictures show that batlike demons sometimes took part in witches' ceremonies.

Bats were also associated with the old stories of vampires that were told in eastern and central Europe. Vampires were the evil spirits of the undead – creatures who rose from their graves at night. In the form of vampire bats, they preyed upon the living by sucking their blood.

Toads were also popular Halloween creatures. They are ugly, small, and scary. They are very common as well. Some toads give off poison, and many people used to believe toads caused warts to grow on human skin. So it was only logical that toads would also be feared as witches' familiars.

Spiders are creepy animals that also have been associated with witchcraft. Some witches were believed to keep spiders to help them work spells. Because spiders are small, it was thought they could easily sneak into places where a person or a larger animal would be noticed. They were therefore perfect for casting spells or for gathering information.

Decorations that show these Halloween creatures are spooky and perfect for holiday parties!

Pumpkins and Jack-o'-lanterns

Black and orange are Halloween colors. Black and orange decorations show how Halloween is connected with nature. Black reminds us that Halloween is a dark and scary night. Plants in the garden die and turn black when autumn turns cold.

The color orange was associated with the ancient Roman harvest festival of Pomona. Wheat and many other crops are light orange when they ripen. So are pumpkins. And the moon sometimes looks orange when it hangs low in the autumn sky.

Pumpkins originated in the New World. They were not grown in the British Isles until the last few centuries. But Ireland gave the jack-o'-lantern to America. The name comes from an Irish story about a man named Jack, who tricked the Devil many times. Because of this, he was forbidden entrance to both heaven and hell.

Jack was condemned to wander in lonely places until Judgment Day. He waved his lantern to lead people from their paths as they walked through shadowy forests, bogs, or marshes. Since pumpkins did not grow in Ireland long ago, the Irish made their jack-o'-lanterns by carving out large turnips or beets.

For many years in parts of England, children have marched through villages on the last Thursday in October. They carry small lanterns called punkies, or punky lanterns. These are jack-o'-lanterns that have been made from large beets, known in rural England as mangels. Experts in religion and folklore tell us the jack-o'-lantern, or punky, represents a human head or skull. The ancient Celts considered skulls to be lucky charms. They could protect people against evil spirits or the power of witches working black magic.

Legend has it that the bright faces of jack-o'lanterns guard against
evil spirits and keep witches at bay.

Fortune-Telling, Parties, and Games

Pictures of witches on broomsticks, black cats, and bats make good decorations for Halloween parties. Grinning jack-o'-lanterns and ghosts or skeletons painted to glow in the dark can give a strange and eerie light. Thread or strings can be hung from the ceiling to look like spiderwebs. Recordings of spooky sounds, screams, and creaking doors can be played to give people chills. It is important to make the atmosphere scary.

Trying to see into the future is an old Halloween game. There are many ways to do it. In earlier times, a young girl would peel the skin from an apple in one piece. Then she threw the piece over her left shoulder. As it fell, it would form the first letter of her sweetheart's name.

Scottish girls believed they could see pictures of their future husbands if they hung wet sheets in front of the fire on Halloween. Other girls believed they would see their boyfriends' faces if they looked into mirrors while walking downstairs at midnight on Halloween.

In some rural places, Halloween is still sometimes called Nut-crack Night. This relates to another old Halloween method of fortune-telling. Two nuts were placed side by side in a crackling fire. The nuts represented a young couple. If one nut suddenly exploded or burst into flame, it meant the love affair would be short-lived. One of the lovers would die, or one of the partners would be untrue. If, however, the nuts behaved the same way in the fire, the match was considered a good one. The young couple would probably marry and be happy together.

In Scotland, young women were sometimes blindfolded and then led out into the garden to pick cabbages. The type of cabbage each girl chose would tell her what her future husband would be like. A green, full head of cabbage meant the man would be young and attractive. A small, white head indicated an old and stingy husband. Cooking the cabbage could carry the predictions a step further. If the cabbage tasted sweet, the husband's disposition would be pleasing. But if the cabbage tasted bitter, then....

In the time of England's Queen Elizabeth I, Halloween was a major holiday. There were fireworks and parties with dancing and games. It was probably during her reign that the tradition of ducking for apples began.

Ducking, or "bobbing," for apples is an old Halloween game. The players usually try to pick up apples floating in a tub of water, using only their teeth. But there are other ways to bob for apples, too. Sometimes the apples are hung by strings attached to a doorway. Or they dangle from the ceiling. Occasionally they are stuck on poles. The trick is to catch the apples as they swing back and forth.

After the games are over, gingerbread, doughnuts, popcorn, and apple cider or hot chocolate are popular things to eat and drink on a chilly Halloween night.

There are other even older Halloween foods. Caulcannon is a bubbling mixture of stewed potatoes, parsnips, and onions. It comes from Ireland where it is still eaten. Fortune-telling objects were put into the dish before it was served. If you found a coin in your portion, it meant you would receive wealth. A ring showed that you would be married soon. A button in the stew meant mixed blessings.

On Halloween in modern Ireland, people also may eat a porridge called sowens. Sowens is made from oatmeal husks. The name sowens is probably related to the Celtic name Samhain. The people also eat a special bread called barmbrack. It contains currants and raisins.

Costumes and Trick-or-Treat

Hundreds of years ago, people wore masks and disguises on Halloween night. They hoped this would help protect them from ghosts and evil spirits. Even today people put on masks and strange costumes.

Grown-ups often dress up and disguise themselves for masquerade parties. Their costumes may be very fancy ones. Sometimes a party may even have a single theme—famous monsters, for example. Occasionally, the theme relates to a certain period in history.

Even if the costume is not elaborate, a mask or special makeup can make someone hard to recognize. There are many kinds of masks. One of the simplest is the black eye mask, called a loup-garou. (The word *loup-garou* means werewolf in French.) This is a mask that forms a band around the eyes and upper face.

Children of all ages dress up on Halloween for parties at school or at home. Very young children dressed up as astronauts, pirates, ballerinas, rock stars, cowboys, or clowns fill the streets. Their parents often go out with them. The trick-or-treaters usually carry big shopping bags to fill up with treats.

"Trick or treat!" is the Halloween cry. Children may go from house to house ringing doorbells. Trick-or-treaters expect to receive a treat—candy, apples, or popcorn. If the children don't get a treat; sometimes they may play a harmless trick. It is important *not* to damage anything or to harm any people or animals. About 100 years ago, Halloween pranks got out of hand and the holiday became known as Mischief Night.

Long ago, people wore costumes at Halloween to scare away evil spirits. Today, children wear costumes to parties and for going trick-or-treating.

The Irish brought the custom of trick-or-treating to the United States. Long ago, the Irish tradition of trick-or-treating began as a ritual of house-to-house begging for food or money in the name of Muck Olla. Muck Olla was a terrifying Celtic god who threatened to destroy the homes and barns of anyone who was not generous enough. People were afraid of the damage Muck Olla might do. They always gave as much as they could. Sometimes, Celtic boys begged people for sticks and logs. They carried this wood to the Druids for them to burn in the Samhain fires.

After Christianity and the observance of All Souls' Day had spread, children still went begging from house to house. Only then they begged for money for soul cakes. Soul cakes were little buns filled with currants or raisins. Eating these cakes was supposed to ease the suffering of those who had died and help them get into heaven.

In France, children begged for flowers to decorate the graves of dead friends and relatives on All Souls' Day. The custom of decorating graves with flowers is a very old one. Archaeologists have found prehistoric graves that date back more than 60,000 years decorated with the remains of flowers.

In some communities today, youngsters collect for charities instead of begging for Halloween treats for themselves. The United Nations Children's Fund—UNICEF—has helped sponsor the program. Youngsters collect useful articles such as soap, toothbrushes, clothing, or shoes. UNICEF then sends these gifts to children in Third World countries. Sometimes they collect money to buy medical goods or other supplies. Halloween has become a time of sharing and not just scaring. Church groups first organized these projects in the 1940s and 1950s.

Dracula's costume has long been a Halloween favorite. Here, the vampire count goes trick-or-treating in black tie and blue jeans.

Who Celebrates Halloween?

Halloween is mostly celebrated in places where the Celts lived long ago, such as in northern France or in the British Isles. It is also celebrated in the United States and Canada. There, people from the British Isles or northern France settled and brought their traditions with them.

For the last 350 years, Halloween has rarely been celebrated in most of England. Some religious people there and in other countries observe October 31 as the eve of All Hallows', or All Saints', Day. Irish, Scottish, and Welsh people, however, have kept some of the old Halloween customs. People from Scotland and Ireland who settled in America and Canada brought their Halloween customs with them.

Even though Halloween customs have died out in most parts of England, recently the holiday has been making a comeback there. For a long time bonfires and house-to-house begging for pennies have been associated with the traditional Guy Fawkes Night. This is the evening of November 5. Guy Fawkes celebrations took the place of Halloween for many years. The holiday had no connection with Halloween, except that it came at the same time of year.

Guy Fawkes was a traitor who plotted to overthrow Parliament, the seat of British government. In 1605, Fawkes and his associates were caught just as they were about to set fire to 36 barrels of gunpowder in the basement of the House of Lords. The whole incident is referred to as the Gunpowder Plot. The traitors were brought to justice and executed in 1606. English people have been celebrating the event each year ever since.

Pumpkin-carving contests like this one in Illinois are a favorite
Halloween activity.

These smiling jack-o'-lanterns float eerily in a California lagoon.

Today, in England, children make straw dummies or figures of Guy Fawkes. They carry them through the streets begging "A Penny for the Guy?" The figures are later burned in Guy Fawkes Day bonfires.

Strangely enough, it was Halloween that originally gave the fire and begging traditions to Guy Fawkes Day. Now, after more than 300 years, the customs are once again returning to Halloween. Many British people are trying to revive the old Halloween customs. They again are celebrating Halloween with costume parties and jack-o'-lanterns and by telling ghost stories.

There are many parts of the world that have never heard of Halloween and its traditions. Still, even in these places, people celebrate All Saints' Day and All Souls' Day. All over the world, wherever there are Christians, the days are major church holidays. In France, Italy, Spain, and South America, All Saints' Day is a holy day.

In some countries, people do things on All Saints' Day or All Souls' Day that are like the early customs connected with the Celtic Samhain. In parts of France, fires are lighted in old stone towers that stand in some graveyards. And in Mexico, children eat candy or cakes that look like grinning skulls, skeletons, and coffins!

There is another strange custom that people follow in some parts of Europe. Many European cemeteries have chapels called bone houses, or charnel houses. Skulls and bones from old graves are piled up in these places. This helps clear the ground so fresh graves can be dug. Sometimes on All Souls' Day, people visit these charnel houses. Often they will stretch out their hands to touch the bones there. This helps people feel closer to their ancestors.

With its fierce eyes and jagged grin, this pumpkin will scare away
both goblins and Halloween tricksters.

Terrifying No More

Halloween costumes are a link with the past. Halloween used to be a holiday of darkness and fear. It meant evil spirits and witchcraft. Ghosts and witches, skeletons and jack-o'-lanterns – all remind us that Halloween was once the most terrifying night of the year. But Halloween is a time that is associated with the powers of saints as well as with the forces of evil. And we no longer have to be afraid. We can now enjoy being just a little bit scared.

Long ago, Halloween was a mysterious and terrifying night filled with unseen dangers. No one takes much of this very seriously anymore. But it helps to make the holiday a little scarier and a lot more fun if you can believe in ghosts and witches for just one night.

Halloween Trivia

An All Souls' Custom in Old Russia

In his novel *The Brothers Karamazov*, the great Russian writer Fyodor Dostoyevski (1821–1881) gives us an interesting look at the folk beliefs of his time. It used to be the custom for Christians in Russia to have the names of departed loved ones remembered at special services for the dead on All Souls' Day. This same custom is followed in the Roman Catholic and Anglican churches even today.

However, a person would sometimes substitute the name of a living person on the list of the names of dead people that the priests read. This was supposed to make the person uneasy. Sometimes a girl would list the name of a sweetheart she hadn't heard from in a long time. The leaders of the church frowned on this practice, however, because they thought it was linked with black magic.

A death's head, like the one carved on this 18th century tombstone, was suppose to protect the soul of the person buried below and prevent the soul from returning as a ghost.

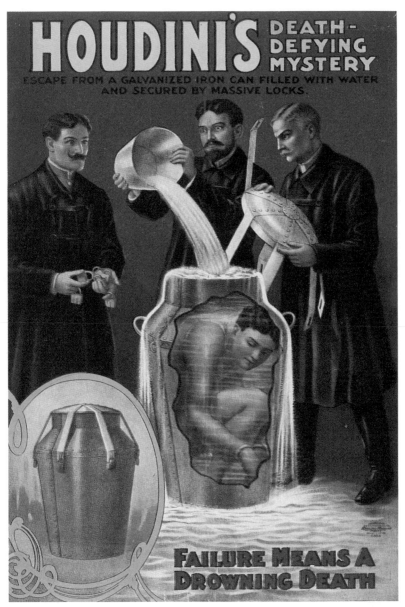

Harry Houdini was famous for being able to escape no matter how tightly he was tied or locked up.

The Halloween Magician

Harry Houdini (1874–1926) was one of the most famous magicians who ever lived. People still don't know the secrets that enabled him to perform some of his greatest tricks.

Strangely enough, Houdini died in 1926 on Halloween night. His death was the result of appendicitis brought on by three stomach punches. A student at a college where Houdini was giving a show had punched the magician. The student was responding to Houdini's challenge to the audience to test how hard his stomach muscles were.

Houdini was a great promoter of spiritualism. This is the belief that certain people, called mediums, are able to talk with the spirits of the dead. Before his death, Houdini promised to return from the spirit world on the anniversary of his death. He would "prove" that spiritualism was real by means of a secret message. To this day, however, no one has yet heard from Houdini's spirit and been able to prove that the message was genuine.

These giant prize-winning pumpkins make a young girl look very small.

The Great Pumpkin

According to *The Guinness Book of Records*, the largest Halloween pumpkin ever measured was grown in 1984 by Norman Gallagher of Chelan, Washington. The pumpkin tipped the scales at an incredible 612 pounds! Since then, even larger pumpkins, weighing well over 700 pounds, have been documented!

An Ancient Greek Festival of the Dead

At the same time of year as the Celtic Samhain, the people of ancient Greece celebrated a week-long festival to honor the ghosts of their dead. This celebration was called Anthesteria. The souls of the dead were said to return from the underworld for the holiday. People held banquets to honor their dead relatives and friends and invited the dead souls to attend. The close of the holiday was marked when the ancient priests clapped their hands and shouted "Be gone, you ghosts! It is no longer Anthesteria!" Anthesteria was much like our Halloween holiday, even though the two celebrations were not related.

Witches' Sabbats and Ancient Religion

Halloween falls exactly six months away from the other great sabbat, on May Eve, or Walpurgisnacht. This is the night before May Day, May 1. This date has been special for witches for centuries – even before Christianity. May 1 is also known as Saint Walpurga's Day. Saint Walpurga was an English nun who went to Germany as a missionary. Saint Walpurga's remains had been moved on May 1. This is why her festival is held on that day. The relics were thought to have miraculous powers. The witches met on the eve of Saint Walpurga's Day, but the saint herself was not connected with witchcraft.

A Halloween Superstition

There is an old wives' tale that used to be popular in eastern Europe. It says that babies who are born with teeth in their mouths (this sometimes happens!) will grow up to be witches or vampires. Stories such as this, along with ghost stories, are hair-raising Halloween favorites.

Witches are remembered on two days during the year—
Walpurgisnacht (the Witches' Sabbat) and All Hallows' Eve.

With the darkness ever growing,
And the moon behind her hat,
You would soon have trouble knowing
Witch is Witch and Witch's Cat.

Which witch is which?

For Further Reading

Barth, Edna. *Jack-o'-Lantern*. New York: Seabury, 1971.
———. *Witches, Pumpkins and Grinning Ghosts*. New York: Seabury, 1972.
Herda, D. J. *Halloween*. New York: Franklin Watts, 1983.
Hierstein-Morris, Jill. *Halloween: Facts and Fun*. Ankeny, Iowa: Creatively Yours Publications, 1988.
Hunt, Roderick. *Ghosts, Witches and Things Like That*. Oxford: Oxford University Press, 1984.
Limburg, Peter R. *Weird! The Complete Book of Halloween Words*. New York: Bradbury Press, 1989.
Sandak, Cass R. *Halloween*. New York: Franklin Watts, 1980.
Walker, Mark. *The Great Halloween Book*. Cockeysville, Md.: Liberty Publishing Company, 1983.

Index